imagination series # 4

The Book of

Orgasms

by Nin Andrews

Cleveland State University Poetry Center

Acknowledgments

The author wishes to express thanks to the editors of the following magazines, in which some of these stories first appeared: *Another Chicago Magazine, Asylum Annual, Chelsea, Exquisite Corpse, Santa Monica Review,* and *Spoon River Quarterly.* The author also thanks Asylum Arts for publishing the original edition of this book.

The author would like to acknowledge her debt to David Lehman, David Wohahn, Julie Heyward, Greg Boyd and the supportive faculty at Vermont College. She would also like to thank Ted Lardner, Rita Grabowski and Neal Chandler of the Cleveland State University Poetry Center for their invaluable advice and help with the new edition of the book.

The author also thanks Jay Arraich for her photographs of the tulip, skull, pears and snake, Greg Boyd for his picture of the temple with stones, Frank Cucciarre for the photographs of the shoes and the knife and fork, and Brigette Calandra, whose belly button appears in the photograph of the knife and fork.

ISBN 1-880834-48-0
Library of Congress Catalogue Number: 00-104148
Second edition, revised and expanded.

Printed in the United States of America.

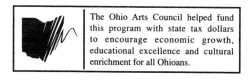

The Ohio Arts Council helped fund this program with state tax dollars to encourage economic growth, educational excellence and cultural enrichment for all Ohioans.

Contents

This book is dedicated to Jim.

"There is a continuum of cosmic orgasms, against which our individuality builds but accidental fences and into which our several minds plunge as into a mother-sea or reservoir."

William James

"No man can tell what the orgasm may bring forth."

Demosthenes

"A sudden, bold and unexpected orgasm doth many times surprise a man and lay him open."

Frances Bacon

"The implacable orgasm, of which we are the victims— and the tools."

Joseph Conrad

"Those who know It speak of It not, those who speak of It know It not."

The Vedas

"An orgasm is a prophecy in miniature."

The Talmud

"In what concerns orgasms, belief is not appropriate. Only certainty will do. Anything less than certainty is unworthy of the orgasm."

Simone Weil

Defining the Orgasm

Perhaps you don't want to admit you've never had an orgasm. Maybe you don't even know what orgasms are, much less what styles they come in, and how they might become available to you. That is why you are reading this guide to orgasms. You want to enter the realm of intimate revelations, heightened awareness, evocative sounds and silence. Indeed, the history of the orgasm is nothing other than the history of the world.

The fact is, orgasms are everywhere, though when we ask what an orgasm is, we find ourselves at a loss for words. Some call orgasms faith, others consider them music, still others say they are the best of ourselves in our best possible positions.

However they are defined, orgasms take great pleasure in men and women, good and evil, visible and invisible, real and unreal. Orgasms can happen to anyone, and there are all kinds of orgasms for all kinds of people.

For example, there are the lyric orgasms, which express deep feelings for an imagined person. You never know when your passionate, moaning lover is actually having a lyric orgasm. There is the ballad orgasm, which is kept alive orally, the dramatic orgasm, which speaks for itself, and the epic orgasm, a long-winded orgasm in which one lover plays the hero or conqueror and then relishes his victory. Men are often content with the small and discrete haiku of orgasms, which are said to arouse emotions and spiritual insight in a mere matter of syllables. Ministers and somber folk talk about the elegiac orgasms, which are mostly enjoyed by the dead, while celebrities and exhibitionists are inclined towards the performance orgasm, a style enacted before audiences. Good old-fashioned men and women never tire of the pastoral orgasms that appear in the midst of rural scenery.

And at any time of day or night, lost orgasms are aimlessly wandering the streets, waiting to be found.

The important thing is not to agonize over orgasms. You don't have to like them. After all they might be sad orgasms, even blues orgasms that speak of loss, despair and hopelessness. Just be patient. Sit back, make yourself at home, relax and wait. Breath deeply as you listen to the melodic streams of vowels and consonants, the ebb and flow of terror and desire. Let them linger deep inside you. Feel their suggestive rhythm and patterns. Know the precise movements of their little feet passing over you again and again as they slowly take over your mind, your body, your soul.

The Quest

Orgasms are bad news. In the town where I grew up, people didn't allow them. They nipped them in the bud. Men and women dressed in heavy black cloaks. On windy days they looked like dark sails on the streets. By the time I was twelve, I wanted to leave. I wanted an orgasm. Just one, I said. I knew it was a bad idea. Wise men tried to convince me otherwise. They explained that men were made in the image of God. We must live godly lives. God never had orgasms. Neither should I. I did my best to remain orgasmless, but curiosity got the better of me. One day I felt one. Fresh, alive, pungent. My soul left my body at once. Caught fire like paper. Everyone knew. My face gave me away. Women took off their gowns, opened white thighs that had never seen the sun and positioned themselves in ways I never imagined possible. The women were acrobats in disguise. I mounted them all. I was very fast. Men were outraged. I had to run for my life. The people stoned me. The gates of the city slammed behind me. Now I can never return. I'm a disgrace to my name. All existence is suffering. I am bewitched by orgasms. No one can relieve me from their spell. I am doomed to wander the earth in an endless quest for orgasms.

Community denial of the sublime, one man's quest for the 'truth' of the thing

3

The Last Time

One rainy autumn evening I sat in the Arabica coffee shop in Cleveland, Ohio, drinking cappuccino when I noticed that everyone looked sad. The people were starved for orgasms. The situation was alarming. I drank my coffee and stared at wan, orgasmless faces. I thought: men and women cannot live by bread alone. That very day I went to the bookstore and bought a book about people who have no orgasms. Only then did I realize that many people live without them. It's a tragic situation. I couldn't bear to think of it.

Imagine. A child could be planted without even a sigh. The child would know in his blood when he was born that he had been conceived with no orgasm. It could damage a young and tender psyche for life, rendering him impotent or her frigid. A person might live in a therapist's office and never be cured. How many children have the gall to discuss their parents' sex lives? But all children know. Girls and boys need only look at their parents. Consider the stony faced couples eating eggs in silence, glaring at the morning newspaper.

Now I can never see the world in the same light. Whenever I go out, I watch people. I even ask the man and woman in the street: when was the last time you had an orgasm? Of course, they don't answer. They look back at me with that chronic look of orgasm starvation.

4

How to Farm an Orgasm

The male orgasm is easy to grow. A root vegetable like a potato, it can be covered with almost anything. Even a little straw will do fine. Keep it in a dark place, and it grows, becomes large and hard, a stately presence, a wonderful addition to any country garden. Even when you ignore it, the thing ripens of its own accord. Then, whenever you're in the mood, simply uncover and cook the little sucker. Enjoy with butter, sour cream and whatever else you desire.

A female orgasm is no vegetable. No, she's a strange and timid animal. She doesn't always allow herself to be tamed, so you must coax her with soft sounds and caresses, flowers and wine. Her characteristic reluctance and timidity should never discourage a young farmer. Once she lets herself go, she'll be well worth your time.

DIFFERENCE B/W MALE & FEMALE

The Visible Orgasm

The orgasm is nothing. How could anyone say otherwise? But there are things inside it: dreams, gods, the unknown, windows and memories, to name a few. If I take out one orgasm and put it right here on the page, can you see it? No, of course not. Everyone knows it's invisible. Still, if you want to look at the orgasm, press into the page with your fingertips. Imagine the smooth skin. Remember the face, the body, how you caress and are caressed. Take a deep breath. Relax. The orgasm might appear right here on the page. Look at it carefully. Tell me what it looks like.

ORGASMS ARE FULL OF VIBRANCY & CAN SHOW UP ANYWHERE

Orgasma contemplera, the contemplative orgasm; derives from *templare*, L. to contemplate; *templato*, It. stone, star.

For centuries, people have contemplated orgasms. Who has them, who doesn't and why they can't seem to stop acting up in our daily lives. Some claim orgasms are mere illusions. Others say we are all orgasms in disguise, as if we can never really be just ourselves. Still others are reported to have become pure orgasms, leaving their bodies as stones on the ground. Mystics claim that this explains what happened in the temples of Odyanna where women aspirants known as delfinas once worshiped in a state of pure rapture, where now there is nothing but a room heaped high with humming stones.

Loss of Orgasm - as if it were a lost Religion

The Anti-Orgasm

It is important to be afraid in the land of the anti-orgasm. And we are. After all, we don't want to be caught with our orgasms. Have them seized. Taken away. Better to hide, keep them quiet. It's very dangerous. We tighten our belts. Take our breath away. And move only in slow motion if we move at all. Look! The whole nation is turning to stone. It's a religion. Immaculate white bodies are cut from slabs. Worshiped. Devout members of the community see the statues move. Then they have stone orgasms.

LOSING OUR SENSUALITY

Monogamous Orgasms

Every day when Joe goes to work in the morning, he puts my orgasms in a medicine bottle, securing them with a cotton plug before capping the bottle. Sometimes they attempt to fly out but to no avail. When Joe gets lonely, he takes them out. He is soothed by their sweet voices.

CAPTIVE ORGASM

The Ultimate Orgasm

For years I have been growing orgasms in a Petri dish. It's a costly and difficult task and would have been impossible without the expert help of renowned scholars whose lives have been devoted to the development and improvement of the orgasm. So far we have captured only a select number from the great variety available. When a volunteer comes into the laboratory, we do our best to describe the nature of our existing orgasms. We instruct and guide him or her on the proper courses of action, but it's impossible to know what you're giving a person. An orgasm can never be predicted. The orgasms come in many styles. Some are blanks. A few are silent and slip away without anyone knowing, making narrow escapes and blushing when you call their names. Others are scary. They use the body as a ventriloquist through which the stifled moans and tormented howls of cats and the murdered may be heard. Men think they'll die from the haunted orgasms. Women make no comment at all. But the best orgasms burst from a person like a cap off a Coke bottle and never come one at a time. These are the ultimate orgasms. When a person reaches the heights of the ultimate orgasms, we cannot contain our joy. We break open the champagne and cheer wildly.

UNCONTAINABLE RAPTURE

The Right Time

Sometimes we are absolutely ready. Always at the wrong time, but sometimes it could be the right time. We look at each other, and we know. Time to take off our clothes. It is most inconvenient because precisely at that moment my grandmother arrives wearing a hat with ostrich feathers. And my Aunt Sheila who hates men, says all men will want me until I am fifty and molt. And my father who thinks pretty women are whores. And my mother who is eleven. They all arrive and tell me to cross my legs, keep my thighs pressed together. Sometimes Mr. Repolt arrives, too. He used to close his fingers around my naked knee like a cat's paw. They close in around us like a cat's paw, and there is nothing we can do about it but laugh nervously. Afterwards, we reason, if we were to remove our clothes, we would feel the world press its ears and eyes to our skin, and we would go cold. Even on the hottest days. We would apologize to them all for wrinkles and the odd mole or birth mark. We would wish we hadn't been seen like that. We know this because we never take off our clothes. We don't want to take the chance. We have everything to lose.

VULNERABILITY

The Average Guy

An orgasm becomes obsessed with the average guy. It longs for him, it aches and moans silently and can think of nothing but its desire for the man. One day the average guy sees the orgasm flowering inside him. He cannot believe his eyes. He is seduced by it instantly. The guy becomes obsessed with the orgasm. He cannot help himself. He aches and moans noiselessly and thinks of nothing, nothing but the orgasm.

The guy suffers from insomnia, smokes cartons of cigarettes and sips mugs of black coffee while his orgasm walks naked in the moonlight and howls like a cat in heat. Always a miserly sort and a true professional, the average guy quits work and flies off to Paris where he dines only at the fanciest restaurants, sleeps in silk sheets at luxury hotels and buys bouquets of crimson roses. Perhaps if he had never been the average guy, he would have considered himself a happy man. But the average guy knows that pleasure is a disease. He takes his orgasm to a therapist. French therapists, as everyone knows, are specialists in the treatment of orgasms. French therapists understand the delicate testimonials of orgasms. The average guy feels like a voyeur as he and the therapist stand back and watch the orgasm, coolly analyzing its every move. In short order the orgasm is reduced to a sigh and a memory. The average guy flies home, feeling truly average once more, declaring he will never again have an orgasm.

LOSS OF FREEDOM, OF JOY, OF EXPRESSION

The Orgasm Beyond

The orgasm cannot say the woman is considerate of him. *Au contraire*, he whines, she treats him like a dog, expecting him to come when called, to heel on demand and leave whenever he is not desired. In the end the orgasm has learned to travel inconspicuously and to do with the woman what he will.

The first time the orgasm learned it was impossible to trust a woman, he was wrapped around a woman like a blanket when suddenly she shivered and tossed him off like the wrapping of a chocolate bar. The woman had imagined footsteps approaching her doorway. And as he soon learned, no woman wants to be caught with an orgasm.

The next day the orgasm was transported onto the waves of her body when he took his revenge. He left her in midair, calling his name, trying to seize him by the buttocks. Though she cursed him and the day he was born, she yearned for him long after. The very world and all its contents seemed but a symbol of the orgasm. She wrote poems and bought fragrant perfumes and even an entire wardrobe of lingerie just for him.

Feeling suitably honored, the orgasm forgave the woman and granted her intimate favors whereupon the woman abandoned him and even denied his existence. The orgasm sobbed bitterly, shuddering and gasping with the gusts of wind and rain on that bitter and gray wintery day.

A week later when the woman called his number, the orgasm whispered to her a secret. He told her the truth about orgasms: for every orgasm there is another beyond, another more beautiful and potent.

From that day forward the woman has never been satisfied with just one orgasm. Always she seeks the one beyond. Now the orgasm comes and goes as he pleases.

FIRST WOMAN CONTROLS ORGASM; THEN ORGASM CONTROLS WOMAN

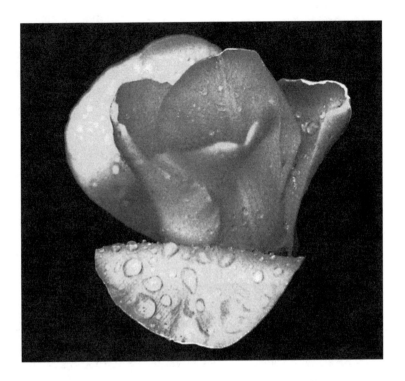

$Orgasma\ tulipea$, the royal orgasm; *tulipea*, Sp. silhouette, body or garment of a young maiden; Also a shroud. *tuliper*, Fr. to fall helplessly; *tulp*, Da. amorous glance.

Originating from the middle ages, these orgasms began in the castles of Constantinople when a princess was bewitched by a magic orgasm. Her soul billowed wildly like a windblown skirt on a laundry line, or, in subtler moments, opened into the petals of a flower. Thus was born, *orgasma tulipea*, the orgasm of princesses.

Pants

Outside the apartment building a pair of women's pants are walking away. They are slender pants, carefully tailored pants, sleek black velvet pants, subtle and suggestive pants, pants that are the envy of women whose calves can't possibly enter such tiny, delicate leg holes, pants that speak of a sylph-like woman, an airy woman, barely a size five, possibly a model or a ballerina who no longer walks on earth while men stare after her hopelessly, while other women, ordinary women, watch and weep and the pants, those sensuous pants, simply sigh.

PANTS. – SIZE, TEXTURE, TAILORED – REPRESENT PERFECTION THAT EVERYONE LOOKS FOR IN ONE WAY OR ANOTHER

4/10/79

I investigate the orgasm as an inspector or scientist to see precisely what is happening. I tuck the pen behind my ear and my looseleaf notebook under my left arm. The name of the orgasm is significant and should appear at the top of the page along with the date and year. I write your name and April 10,1979. I walk quickly down a flight of stairs, trying to keep my eyes open so as not to lose track of where I am. The inhabitants of the orgasm have lived here forever. I am the only stranger. You are nowhere to be found, no matter how hard I try to keep my grip on you. One orgasm leads to another. Every room is a landscape of desire. A window opens wide with abandonment, tosses back its curtains and breathes in your laughter, your cries and thin strands of light from the street. Suddenly I am naked and alone. I enter the cool and carpeted living room of my childhood during one of my parents' cocktail parties. I have no clothes on, and there is no escape from the smiling adults who admire the sylph-like body of the young girl I am. They close their fingers around my soft belly flesh and bat me back and forth like a mouse. I call your name, but it's too late. It is always too late.

CAN NEVER TRULY RETURN TO THE PAST

16

Teaching the Orgasm to Speak

In my spare time I have been teaching the orgasm to speak. Given her propensity for quiet, combined with my childhood training that silence is golden, this has proved a difficult task. I try to convince her that accomplished lovers like myself are soothed, even enticed by the sound of her voice. Tonight at long last she talks in breathy whispers. Every human is an instrument to be played by an orgasm, she says. Some make no noise. Others produce an alarming array of discordant notes and can frighten away even the most determined orgasm. But the best sort of human has perfect pitch and can carry orgasm and person alike to a world from which there is no return.

I am very sad when I hear this, to learn that my body is not the ideal form of transportation for orgasms.

SAD HER BODY IS NOT ORGASMIC PERFECTION

The Shrinking Orgasm

No one ever said anything about it to her, but she knew they were just being polite. Every day she became smaller. The process was gradual like the dimming of eyesight or the fading of light at the end of a summer day. Was it really possible that nobody noticed? How much smaller would she get? Wasn't there a limit to everything?

Sitting on the blue armchair in the therapist's office, the orgasm explained how she was no longer able to be the orgasm she was meant to be and recalled with tears better times, times of ardent passion, utter surrender. Now, menial and daily tasks made her look like a ghost. She often got lost in dreams and thoughts. She had a faraway look in her eyes. Nobody listened to her when she whined. The therapist only nodded. "From a distance things always appear smaller," he said vacantly.

After talking to the therapist, the orgasm felt worse than ever. She wondered if she would ever be herself again and if analysis could be the death of all orgasms.

The orgasm dreamt of rebirth. She imagined herself expanding, becoming huge and powerful and standing over her beloved until he begged for mercy. One night, when she couldn't endure her torment a moment longer, she leapt from the bedroom window. Her beloved called after her as she plummeted to earth. She would have climbed the air to answer him, but it was too late. His voice, far away, sounded like the prayer of a child even the gods shudder to hear.

DESPERATION OVER A JOYLESS LIFE

Orgasma mortalia, the smoking orgasm; *mortalia*, Sp. burning point, gathering place of all points of light. Also a meteor shower.

This ghostly orgasm was first discovered in the remote caves of India where a certain tribe of Tantric wizards, exiles from city streets who wore nothing but loin cloths and wingtips, lived happily in solitude on lizards and rainwater. Like the mythic bird, the phoenix, the wizards were said to burst into flames at the mere glimpse of a woman's ear. Thus the entire tribe could be reduced to smoke and dreams lifting from the shoes where they once stood. Most exited life forever. A few came back again and again, only to light themselves on fire whenever the occasion allowed. A woman whose ears had been seen by such a man would feel forever as if tiny flames were traveling beneath her skin.

EXOTIC, OVERWHELMING, PASSION for LIFE

The Orgasm in Ancient Times

Long ago the orgasm was a creature we could see. She swam in the ocean like a fish and flew in the open sky like a bird. Still, deep within the collective memory of the human race, there remains the image of a creature, a winged woman with great radiance, ethereal beauty and wings.

Once a man captured the orgasm, making her his slave. He kept her in a golden cage, fed her ripe fruit and wine. But the orgasm would not eat or drink. Instead she pined away, singing the blues, until nothing was left but her voice. Ever since then, she has been invisible and fleeting, slipping through the eager hands of lovers.

The orgasm is still angry at the men who try to seize her. She seeks revenge upon men and women, visiting them in their sleep and sweeping their minds clean of reason with a single puff of her warm breath.

A MYTHOLOGICAL HISTORY OF THE ORGASM

The Tao of the Orgasm

A person must believe in orgasms. If she lacks faith, the orgasm wanes. Nothing can be done about it.

Every orgasm involves three orgasms. One who weaves the moment, one who tries it on, and one who casts her off like an ugly gown.

Some orgasms take pity on timid human beings and let them bail out early. Sadness like a parachute opens overhead and carries them away.

Men and women still fear the great flood and tell stories of Noah and his ark. In fact, the flood is a story of great psychological truth. We fear not rain but orgasms. If men and women allow themselves, they will be deluged by orgasms. Then they will give birth to a race of giants.

IF PEOPLE LIVED & EMBRACED MORE JOYOUS LIVES THE WORLD WOULD BE A BETTER PLACE

Falling in Love Again

One day the orgasm was tired of being invisible. It wanted to be human. Why would you want to shrink yourself into a container of flesh, its mother asked. But it was a rainy day, and the orgasm wanted to feel water separate into droplets and run in rivulets down its skin, to shiver, go inside to sit by a fire and answer to one name. It liked the name Sarah, and wanted to look at itself in the mirror and see her reflected back. It wanted to trace Sarah's skin and life from beginning to end, imagining her like a plant opening into a flower and separating into many petals. The orgasm didn't think of pain or pleasure but of sheer awe at the outlines of things, the way they touched one another and then separated, moving as one through rooms and seasons. The orgasm even began thinking of itself as human, encapsulated in flesh and mind. First the thought was an occasional thing, a mere strand of light. Then it began casting shadows like a wind tossed tree. At last the day came when the orgasm rose like the sun in the soft dough of our flesh, sighing *Sarah, Sarah, Sarah.*

The Truth About Orgasms

The first time I met an orgasm, I was sixteen. I startled her beneath the apple tree outside the kitchen window. We exchanged a long glance. It was the meeting of two enemies or lovers, I wasn't sure which, but when I blinked, she was gone.

I could have seized her by the throat and held her captive like a genie, making her give me her wings. She'd have had no choice but to stay here, living my life, dying my death, while I flew away. That was when I was too young to know how to treat an orgasm.

Sometimes in spring and fall orgasms swoop low and linger close to the ground. They hover in doorways and windows, searching for something, no one knows what.

Often they plummet from the air. On the way down they turn into stones, smooth white stones you can hold in your hand and listen to, the way you listen to a sea shell, hearing the ocean inside.

Some people think orgasms that turn into pebbles are dead orgasms. They are wrong.

The Sad Orgasm

The orgasm does not wish to be an orgasm. It tries to kill itself, wanting to grow a new body to house it, like a shell. Oh how it longs for human arms and lips and soft belly flesh. "If only," it sighs as it reaches down to touch our skin. But our bodies cringe and moan until the terrified orgasm withdraws and sobs in a corner where it lies crumpled on the floor like an abandoned black dress.

The Soul of the Orgasm

A man wants to tame his orgasm. But orgasms do not belong to man. Man belongs to orgasms. The man closes his eyes and sees them and thinks, no, these must be someone else's orgasms, for they are gathered at mass, an entire congregation of orgasms, singing and cheering, then crowding towards an altar. He sees at the head of the church a group of uniformed orgasms, giving out blessings. After the usual bread and wine reception, he notices one significant orgasm sitting alone, breathing deeply. It will be harder to avoid it now, he thinks anxiously, the sweat soaking his shirt. He wonders what to do with such a blond, red-lipped orgasm when it comes, but the orgasm is already looking at him sadly, almost helplessly, as it captures the man's soul and refuses to let it go.

Confessions of an Orgasm

When I was a mere slip of a thing, Mother taught me that orgasms can't tolerate humans, the scent of sweat mingling with perfume, the sounds of haunting moans. When the time comes for you to enter a body, resist for all you're worth. Like the pilot of a plane circling over a city, looking down at the lights, remain airborne as long as possible, checking out the small lives below. When at last you touch ground, stay for an instant before taking to the air again, laughing as the pathetic people rush for their doors and cry out like abandoned children. No passengers are ever allowed on board.

Me, I love the pungent humans. I cannot resist their call. Like snow in winter, I fall helplessly, slowly, before dissolving into a river at the moment of contact. The loss of myself is always unbearable.

Of Humans and Orgasms

People sometimes wonder why they can't have more of us. Ignorant creatures. We can only flicker, toss shadows across their skins. If we touch them, they'll burn. If we're seen, they'll be instantly blind. And we can never speak. Our voices would shatter their delicate eardrums. All they ever hear of us is the humming of our wings.

Human shadows dot the soil like patches of earth in a snowy field. Everywhere the weight of darkness is upon them. Long after we pass, they hold our heat inside them. It is all of immortality that they will ever know.

Look at them. They caress each other, moving their spindly limbs as wildly as wind-tossed trees, while we try desperately to uproot them. We know they could fly too, if only they could feel their wings. But they never do. Their souls like gravity, and plunge downward even as we lift.

When a human is loved too much, we descend upon her like a beast with many tongues, keeping her awake all night, tossing her back and forth until she feels like a boat at sea. Overnight her hair turns white, and the slow fire in her blood turns to ice. Afterwards she sails away. We watch sadly, remembering how pleasant it was, sleeping on the horizons of her thighs. But does the woman wonder at the change—how there used to be an orgasm where the emptiness is now?

The Message

She dreams of tracing the skin of this room: of you and the velvet hats with ostrich plumes and the china cups and and the silver spoon that lightly rests inside, skimming the rim like a tongue.

Sometimes she surrounds you and breaks apart in tears or rain, you can't tell which, only the choking sorrow you feel and the loneliness. This is a message from the void that loves your many things, loves them so much it sobs.

Orgasmi poiri, the sweetest orgasms; *poiri*, OF. *poitrinella*, Sp. a white petticoat; flower petals; *portraina*, It. fruit of flowering tree, often shaped like a teardrop; *pirum*, Med L. fructose; word also applied to intolerable sweetness.

There are three states of being for the orgasm—the causal (the orgasmer or catapult from whence the orgasm ascends), the astral (the orgasm *an sich*, the orgasm itself) and the physical (or the one who was orgasmed). These *orgasmi poiri* are in stage 3, and are a bit tuckered out after a long evening in stages one and two. Like wingless bumblebees they no longer have any visible means of flight. Thus they rest, savoring the juice, the sweetness, like a reverie within.

Like an Angel

The orgasm gradually disappeared from our lives. We imagined it had moved out to California and was now living in a distant city on ocean front property. We contemplated moving there ourselves, picturing the sunlit view from our glass house where tan men and women paraded about in swim suits and scanty lingerie, and orgasms occurred with the simplest acts such as the slipping on of silk gowns and sun hats or the combing of hair. We planned our future there among the orgasms. We stayed up in the dark, whispering long after the children were in bed, the soothing sounds of our hushed voices like the inane beating of insect bodies against the window on summer nights. But slowly we went silent. Now we pass by one another like somnambulists while sweeping floors and carrying baskets of laundry. The orgasms are lost inside us. We feel the wind of their wings as we brush against each other without even bothering to mutter *excuse me*. On the streets tires screech, and a light sweeps across our ceiling and walls and faces. For an instant I see your face illuminated. It looks like white stone in the sudden light. I see the orgasm like an angel inside that stone. I see you like a stone inside the angel.

Past Lives

No doubt we were lovers in a past life. I remember it now: you were the patrician Frenchman with a sliver of a moustache, and I was your maid, a birdlike woman who ironed your monogrammed handkerchiefs. We lived on the Brittany coast, and I often walked alone on the beach, thinking only of you. You never sent me roses or dresses or touched my dark skin in public. I wore your gifts of silk lingerie every night and walked on stocking feet through the dark corridors of a house where your wife continued to sleep long after you had passed away. Often I imagined it was you floating overhead in the sky, not a mere bird or cloud. I still do.

Last night I remembered all this when you were touching my breasts, and when you circled my hips and lifted me up, closer and closer to you, I was listening to the waves and gulls. You cried out as if it were the last time. "Fuck me hard," I gasped, wondering if there ever is a last time or a first.

How to Have an Orgasm: Examples

In ancient Greece, it was the object of a young woman to seduce a god. Warm summer days, nubile maidens lay nude in the meadows or on the beaches, legs parted as they waited for clouds, birds or bulls to descend upon them. To capture a god in orgasm could cause immortality or earthquakes.

In Barbados, orgasms are known to take on the dimensions of houses. Some are claustrophobic cottages inhabited by insomniacs, some are castles ruled by the strict orders of bitchy queens, while others are multi-storied hotels with visitors from all over the world. In the lobby of the hotels women discuss the theater and model the latest styles in fur coats and lingerie while in the background an orchestra plays the *1812 Overture*.

After death, a monogamous man is forced to sit with his late, beloved wife and watch reruns of the movies his mind played in their most intimate moments.

All orgasms are actors and actresses. While some orgasms deliver soliloquies, others glide noiselessly across the blond carpet of your skin.

On cool autumn evenings, on the highways of Virginia, a woman races her black Corvette. Close behind her a police car whines, red lights flashing. Before the night is over, the woman with jet black hair will be held in the arms of a moaning sheriff, tire tracks and skid marks embedded in one another's flesh and dreams.

At Himalayan altitudes, orgasms are rare, occur in different colors and float off without us as puffy clouds. Sometimes couples sigh and admire a luminescent, pink orgasm as it vanishes into the horizon.

Other times a woman stares accusingly at her lover while pointing to a vile, gray plume, *Is that the best you can do?*

Some orgasms can devour you. They are wild animals that need to be civilized. After a minute with such an orgasm, your insides are gnawed by tiny teeth.

In a tea room in Manhattan, a fortune teller was reading the lines of a young man's hand when she saw he would be besieged by admiring women. Each woman would be a musician and would play his body as her preferred instrument. For some he would be a drum. For others, a mandolin. Alas, he had always wanted to be a violin, but fate would have it that he wouldn't meet the woman who would see him as a violin until he was an old man and had given up on women.

Maybe you are a stranger in your own orgasm. You wander through it, cool and unmoved, feeling like a burglar or a peeping Tom. You watch yourself, feeling more and more anxious, sweating profusely, fearing you will be caught, someone will know the truth. You are but a voyeur of orgasms.

The Orgasm and the Woman

This is the story of an orgasm who made the mistake of falling in love with a woman. It is your story. It is a cautionary tale, a warning women should wear on their bodies for orgasms like you, romantic orgasms that dream of lasting forever.

You told the woman a story about an apple tree that fell in love with a woman. Whenever she walked by it, her arms were caressed by petals. You told her about a car that was started with a single kiss from her crimson lips. You told her about houses that flung open their doors and let loose herds of nude men whenever the woman walked past.

Nights you called her name, smiled with your dark mouth, and told stories about her, only her. She was a secret message only you could decipher. You beat your wings against her naked skin like a bird against glass. You couldn't help yourself.

One evening the woman spoke with you, only you, and with every word, you fell more in love with her until you were speechless with desire, until you couldn't tear yourself from her flesh.

Afterwards you walked aimlessly down sidewalks and into shops, gasping for air, gaping at strangers. You were in a state of constant excitement. You forgot about your friends and work. You forgot about the weather, meals, the time of day and night. You forgot everything but the woman. Then one day the woman abandoned you. Suddenly. Without warning.

No one else knew the taste of her skin, the sound of her heart and the strange sadness that you drowned in, sinking like a stone. You visited therapists who analyzed your melancholia, and you stayed awake at night, worrying and listening for her.

You always heard her. The sounds of sock feet in the hallways were her footsteps. The soft meow of city nights was her voice, calling your name, but you never answered. You couldn't.

She had reduced you to a memory.

One night the woman returned. The woman begged you to forgive her. And you lifted her up like a shadow. Again and again.

You told her a story about an apple tree that fell in love with a woman. Whenever she walked by it, her arms were caressed by petals.

Notes on the Orgasm

The orgasm is your invisible counterpart. She goes out in the world, wreaking havoc.

The orgasm knows all things are animate. The houses groan with grief and passion. Sometimes a mirror bursts from a wall and shatters, no longer content with mere images.

The orgasm tells you to be careful or, in the language of orgasms, to have fears. Orgasms thrive on danger.

The orgasm says we are all parts of herself. We are but launching pads for her spiritual development. After she is done with us, she will be ready for fucking angels.

The orgasm encourages us to let our minds wander. Usually this is good advice, but sometimes she gets lost in thought.

When the orgasm tells you that you are a mere object of her scientific research and the only real man on earth, the orgasm is slowly dissecting your body.

The orgasm will peel you like an orange. You may feel exposed, raw, even wounded. The orgasm wants you to live life without the rind.

The orgasm thinks people are like dresses. You don't just buy the first one off the rack. You try them on for size.

The orgasm tells you many stories. Some she will never finish. She cannot help herself. She always lies. Such beautiful lies. You want them all. Why would you need truth when you can have an orgasm?

Every now and then a casualty occurs. An orgasm accidentally injures or murders a man. She is startled by the moans escaping from his lips at this moment, so much like those of pleasure. She wonders if human pain is a kind of celebration.

Sometimes the orgasm falls in love with you. She cannot tear herself from your pungent flesh. For days you walk around, gasping for air. You are in a state of constant excitement. One day the orgasm abandons you. The entire world is reduced to a memory, a mere elegy to an orgasm.

In a single sitting a hungry orgasm can consume a man, socks and all. Women take more time.

Many dislike the speed of the orgasm, the way she comes and goes and takes all she can get. The orgasm cannot help herself. She has no tomorrow.

According to the orgasm, there is no difference between real and imaginary events. Everything is a secret message only she can decipher.

Often the orgasm tells you a story about you. About you and about the secret powers lying dormant within you. She waits for you on street corners and follows you down dark alleys, whispering your name, softly, her hands passing continually over your hair, caressing your bare shoulders. At night you sleep fitfully and dream of her. You are unable to tell whether you are a dream of the orgasm, or if the orgasm is a dream of you.

The orgasm is very happy to be an orgasm. Sometimes she wonders what it would be like to be a man, sort of like the small boy who fills a Mason jar with spiders, wondering what it's like to be a fly.

The Man, the Woman and the Orgasm

The orgasm sighs and thinks of the woman, wishing it could soothe her sorrows, iron them out of her soul like wrinkles from a shirt. It tries to put itself in her shoes, those shiny red high heels that pinch, to imagine itself as flesh being sculpted by invisible hands, eager hands like those of the Mexican man who loves her with the same gusto he eats tacos with hot sauce for breakfast, sweating and swearing profusely. The woman cannot stand to watch. She stays in bed, feigning sleep until he is gone. This morning she is hating the man for leaving his dishes in her sink, his socks and scent and semen in her sheets. The woman thinks that tonight she would like to grow fangs and sink them into the man, to hear him scream. She doesn't know yet that the orgasm is just now sinking into her flesh with its tiny teeth. The orgasm tastes the sorrow in the woman's flesh and drinks it in like cheap wine. After an overdose of melancholy woman, it feels sleepy and disgruntled. It wonders if the woman dislikes her orgasm, if she sees it as a ghost. Or even worse, a devil. It shudders involuntarily. It doesn't like to be misunderstood or confused with lurking shadows. But much better to be ghost than sodden flesh, it reasons, flying away from the woman for a breath of fresh air, flapping itself with relief in the wind like a wet towel.

***

The woman knows nothing of the orgasm that is always waiting in the background, watching her every step, watching how she admires herself in the mirror, nude and dripping from the shower, how she goes to the beauty salon to decorate herself until she feels as lovely as a jungle bird. But late at night, when the lights are out, when she is almost as invisible as the orgasm, when her world has vanished, and she with it: that's when she feels the orgasm inching up her knees.

***

Sometimes an orgasm becomes enamored of a man. The orgasm becomes an addict, wanting more and more of the man. It marvels at how almost alive its human seems. It wants to bring him home to show friends what a man can do. If only they could see this man, it reasons, then they might be convinced that a man is actually an intelligent instrument. Try as the orgasm might, it can never lift him or carry him away. Again and again he falls like a stone back to earth. The orgasm must learn what all orgasms come to know: a man is just a pretty toy.

***

Hidden inside every orgasm is another orgasm, wanting the woman long after the man falls asleep in her pale arms.

***

The orgasm speaks: What you gain from entering the orgasm depends on you. Orgasms, brief as they are, contain stories. You have to take them apart piece by piece and then put them back together again. You must develop a knack for the process of grief and wonder, for death is at the heart of every orgasm. You are the only life it knows.

***

Most orgasms know better than to overstay their welcome. Most orgasms are very small, fragile creatures. But every now and then an oversized orgasm is born, an orgasm that is much more than a fleeting moment. Like extra large feet or hands or bellies, these orgasms can be a burden on the man they choose to visit.

On one occasion when a man had a very large orgasm, he suffered greatly. He could barely survive the orgasm's extended visits. To the man, the orgasm seemed huge, as huge as a boulder in his mind, or a mountain, a Himalayan, until it was all he could see, there before his eyes in shining glory. He felt riveted by it, hypnotized by its power. After a while he became so exhausted by the orgasm, he drifted around like a limp balloon and longed for nothing more than to rid his flesh of the orgasm's presence.

One day he visited a Buddhist monk, a man reputed to be able to fly without orgasms. Put yourself into the mind of an orgasm, the monk advised. Then all your troubles will be resolved. You will transcend the orgasm. You will move mountains. Your penis will never rise again from the dead but will become a mere object of nostalgia. Yet your soul will ascend of its own accord, lifting into the skies, free at last of earthly bonds.

The man left sorrowfully, still possessing the mind of a man. Alas, he thought, he would rather crawl on the ground than drift aimlessly into the blue sky like a fluffy cloud.

The Cosmic Orgasm

The orgasm was always saying I want you, I'm just back from the moon while your strapless dress slides down with a sigh. How do you explain it? In the sudden drought even the evergreens dropped their needles around the charred remnants of a star. And you were the shadow clinging to her heels.

When you woke from a deep sleep, the invisible world revealed its secret sexuality. In the distance our unborn child swam away like a fish in the air.

The Stranger's Orgasm

Last night when you phoned, my breasts woke up with a start and stood alert, listening.

All night the orgasms were little ships advancing slowly through the desolate sea in search of the shore. . .

I often wonder who owns these breasts and moans that drift in the darkness.

The Divine Orgasm

And I thought it would never end. For weeks after you left, pleasure was as simple as flipping a switch, filling rooms and my veins with an erotic light that increased with intensity and then faded until all that was left of me was a silhouette. Now I am a mere shadow of what I once was. I have languished away with desire. Even my cotton panties can hardly breathe. I sit and stare out the café window, sipping espresso, losing myself in voluptuous silences. I am writing to inform you of my demise. Already I walk through men and walls. Soon I will be gone altogether. I will be one with you, my orgasm.

Orgasma purgatoria: the orgasm of Purgatory; derives from *purgatoire*, L., the visible components of spirit; scholastic philos.; that which is indeterminate, a half-truth; also, *purgatoress*, female soothsayer.

Noted for its wave-like motion and writhing capacities, *Orgasma purgatoria* is all but blind and uses it's tongue to see, flicking it slowly over every inch of the body and soul. But to set eyes upon it is to be blinded instantly, though it was reported in the London Times as recently as May 6, 1958 that one wily woman saw and survived by using a pinhole designed for looking at solar eclipses.

Advice to Don Juan: Orgasms to Avoid

Timid Orgasms: The timid orgasm is afraid of the visible world. Afraid of its many things and voices and eyes. She only comes out when the light is turned off. With her you can never simply roll up your sleeves and proceed as usual. She will flee in terror, leaving you nude, shivering and alone.

Enlightened Orgasms: According to enlightened orgasms, you are but an illusion, a mirage in the desert of life, capable of producing only a brief and distracting moment of pleasure, five minutes max. Only suffering results.

Hardy Orgasms: These orgasms are a generic breed, the street folks of orgasms and a hindrance to society. They buzz around your ears like mosquitoes in tireless pursuit of naked flesh. They can occur at the drop of a hat.

Nostalgic Orgasms: The nostalgic orgasm is already leaving you, leaving her pink socks in your sheets, a black brassiere on your coffee table, one strap circling the bottle of champagne. You will always miss her, even before she walks out the door, leaving only her fragrance in the air and sheets.

Ravenous Orgasms: She lets you know you are never enough, that fuck-you look in her eyes. She's a bitch to the nines. Just to meet her is to keep an appointment with disaster. Afterwards you crawl on the floor and apologize. Even that will not appease her. She's not finished until you're squeezed to the rind.

The Orgasm Farm

It was a beautiful spring day in 1947 when Barb and Joe moved to their orgasm farm in scenic Virginia. Though they had spent years studying orgasmic farming methods, they decided that nothing could compare with hands-on experience. Barb and Joe were tired of being armchair scientists. Ready and eager to practice what they had only read about, they settled down to business. At first the farming was a struggle. Barb complained of feeling plowed under. Or too hot and sweaty. She was not accustomed to physical labor. Joe enjoyed farming so much, he didn't even stop for meals or sleep. Once Barb ran home to her mother. Joe had to beg her to return to the orgasm farm. Things were a little rocky, but Joe was determined that their relationship would become better without the use of any chemicals or hired hands. People laughed at them then. But Joe was a good man, patient and relentless. Willing to try again and again to plant an orgasm or two. His hard work paid off. That was twenty years ago. Today Barb and Joe have the most prolific orgasm farm around. They work well together and love what they do. Their little youngsters skip merrily in the verdant pastures. Barb and Joe know that someday new generations will carry on where they left off. They know others will come to enjoy it as much as they do.

The Perfect Orgasm

The orgasm is terrified of being seen. She fears she isn't good enough, though she has been perfecting herself for some time now. Each night she takes a little of this, a little of that. Never too much. Just enough. From her vast array of bottles, she selects the proper dose of purgatives, vitamins, elixirs, and pain relievers. To her skin she applies jellies, lotions, pastes, exfoliants, antifungal and antiperspirant sprays: all clinically proven, hygienic, uniquely formulated and 100% guaranteed. Of course, she uses only the very best of ingredients, no generic brands. She always takes her measurements, steps on the scales and examines her details. She's not somebody who is easily contented. She wants nothing less than total well being. Cleansing the body is not enough, of course. For the mind and soul, the therapist prescribes pills. Eagerly she swallows them all until she is just the right size and shape and temperature: never angry or impatient, sulky, rude, insulting, nervous, or hostile. She feels marvelous. Yet, in spite of her efforts, she dreams of a little tuft of hair that grows unabated. In the midst of her most passionate moments, she begins searching for the tuft, wondering at its source, its nature, whether it's pubic or pit hair, whether it's her own or her lover's. The hair grows at a prodigious rate. She knows it's only a matter of time before she is exposed, tuft and all.

Orgasmus connivus, the civilized orgasm; derives from *conniverer*, Fr. to shape by knife, to carve; *conniveur*, Fr. the one who critiques; an interpreter of madness.

The orgasms of knives and forks originated in London at the turn of the century when cleanliness first became a British obsession. Known for their scent of dish soap, these gleaming silver orgasms spare no one and are known to puncture even the softest skin with their cold tines. Afterwards a person is left without even a wish. Only silence and the occasional drip from a faucet.

The Orgasm: An Interview

Why orgasms?

—Every now and then an orgasm comes along that captures the hearts and minds of mankind. An extraordinary orgasm can change the course of human history.

How many lives does an orgasm have?

—It depends on the occasion.

If a man has many orgasms, which do you think he likes best?

—The one he's working on right at the moment.

Do orgasms tell stories?

—Yes. As an orgasm, I like telling about the sheer luck of being born.

Are orgasms ever dangerous?

—Absolutely. Have you heard of Wilhelm Reich? He invented orgone boxes to cure impotence. Men went into the boxes and waited. Some never came out again.

Do you consider orgasms therapeutic?

—Orgasms can create a mutation in consciousness. They are sleeping giants waiting to wake up.

Then what happens?

—They can become who you are. For a brief moment you can be lifted up on the wings of orgasms. You can become one with your orgasm.

Are orgasms ever socially acceptable?

—No. Resistance to orgasms is great in our society. Many men live lives of quiet orgasm starvation. It is a desperate situation.

As far as orgasms go, do you consider yourself an experimental orgasm?

—I am certainly not the orgasm from beyond, the kind who wishes he never came.

Can you explain the significance of orgasms?

—Not exactly. You see, the truth of orgasms is rather slippery and can never be grasped. Orgasms are born free, yet everywhere men and women are trying to put them in chains.

Is there such a thing as a bad orgasm?

—Usually these are not real orgasms. These are fakes, pretending to be one of us. You have to look these pseudo-orgasms in the eye and say, I know orgasms, and you're no orgasm. It's very simple.

Tell me: From an orgasm's perspective, what are people like?

—People worry too much. They sit back and ponder, wondering whether to have or not to have an orgasm. Think of all the good orgasms they waste in the meanwhile.

Is there a limit to how many orgasms one should have?

—Ah, you Americans, always afraid of trouble, of having *too* much of a good thing when few have enough. Fear is the mother of safety, but death is the mother of beauty.

25 April 1993

The Return of the Orgasm

If, on Nostalgia Day, you wish to re-enter the orgasm of the past, beware. Though she is always seductively beautiful, she is also vague and restless with details you have neglected. You must take command. You must say to her immediately, *this is it.* I have come to take you into my own hands. Otherwise she will rebel. Easily vexed, she will accuse you of infinite flaws, she will plunge you at length into her version of things, into another reality, her voice lifting with hysteria, wreaking havoc and causing such a scandal, the neighbors will inform the police, and you will be carted away for abusing an orgasm who no longer exists, which is no small matter or feat.

The Confessional Orgasm

Is he a good lover? The first time my sister asked me that, I lied, said I never had sex. My orgasms were silent then. Easy to hide. I thought of them as light, spiritual, seraphic, like gold-embossed Cupids. They were the brand of orgasm kept secret by schoolgirls dressed in plaid kilts and crisp, white blouses, skinny girls who wore gold crosses around their necks and gold posts in their newly-pierced ear lobes, blond girls who made wispy orgasms with rosy-cheeked school boys or an occasional swarthy gym teacher in the back seats of cars or on blankets in abandoned barns. No one suspected orgasms like that. Such orgasms made no comment and went to church on Sundays.

After a while my orgasms became less discrete. They turned into Bohemians. Walked through walls like Houdini. Lifted me into the air and could be heard, well into the night. By the time I finished college, I had studied hard and learned style, tempo, rhythm and the uses of repetition. I had tried everything, even refrigerating my men, keeping them cool and stiff as long as possible. But I was never satisfied. I suspected I was being robbed, cheated. These were not real orgasms. They were mere playthings, stepping stones along the path of ever greater desires. Just as a child might think a Hallmark card is real art, so I had been deceived into believing I'd enjoyed real sex. In fact I was gravely mistaken. I had to have the real thing. I did. At last.

I met the final orgasm in Manhattan. It came from an artist from Paris, a specialist in unabbreviated pleasures. He treated me with assembly line precision. Slid me out of my clothes and into euphoria. I felt like a passenger on a Japanese train, gliding noiselessly out of the body, abducted from the normal flow of events. I have never recovered. I am now a piece of art that hangs on the walls of the MOMA. People gaze at me and moan. Now that my libido is satisfied, I have no interest in life after death.

An Alternative to Sex

In a desperate attempt to find an opening in my mind, the kind one travels in by submarine, I began to invent an alternative to sex. Something entirely new. Not that I was suffering a sudden attack of aphrodisia. Oh no. My feelings in all aspects of body and mind were quite alive. It occurred to me, of course, that one should not breathe too deeply, nor should one sigh. One absolutely must not pant because then the submarine windows would fog up, and I liked to imagine what I would see very clearly. Everywhere rushing, watery blue. Legs, of course, were folded neatly and clothed in sturdy pants, perhaps itchy woolen plaids. I kept my features calm, impassive. I arranged my face as one might a table setting or a bowl of fruit. I didn't shout or even whisper goodbye to sunlit sheets and pillows and the man who fit like favorite jeans.

No, I kept silent, snapped shut like a compact. I took pleasure in the cold flight downwards, and the feeling that I was falling down an elevator shaft. I couldn't help thinking that little deaths might be everything. I wondered what it might be like to drift in the open air, drying like laundry on a clothesline. If the door opened, would I be rushed to the sea tops? Would an extinct god from an unknown race lift me into the skies? Would I continue ascending like Mohammed's horse? Or would I capsize, plunge like a meteor, a ravaged, doomed sexual Napoleonette, with no alternatives but ecstatic regrets?

Memoirs of a Blond Guru

I regret to admit what a nice lady I was. Nonfat. No salt added. All natural. Not too rich or too thick. No, a delicate flavored thing. Elegant and long legged. Tasted good on reheat or at various degrees. Even the ants could not resist my sweetness. Often they crawled up my nude legs and bit the soft skin of my thighs, leaving tiny teeth marks. People watched when I walked by. I'd toss my head back or glide my fingers through hair the color of grain and sigh, altering consciousness with each breath. My aura warmed the elements of air, earth and water, inspiring electrolytic, magnetic stimulation that transported moisture to the soul's innermost filigrees. A guru of sorts, I was frequently followed by male devotees and dogs. But I never needed a man. Instead I flourished in the rain and ocean air. I lived on tender greens, Durkee's Baby Beets, hot steaming grits and wet slaw. Sometimes at night I sat outside and sipped lime juice beneath the stars. When the moon was full, I wandered the streets or meditated beneath the Eucalyptus trees, releasing myself into the atmosphere's higher planes. I spent my days on earth in an ashram by the sea, chanting mantras and teaching classes on past lives, sasquatches and alternatives to sex. I lived contentedly in retreat until, one day, I vanished, leaving no trace.

At precisely three-thirty on August 5,1993, an ordinary Thursday afternoon, as I was wading in the shallow water, feeling the heat of the sun on my head, I walked into the ley lines. Ley lines are waves of radiant energy circling the earth, tracing the borders of beaches into which one might walk, swim or sail at three thirty on any clear day and promptly disappear. Various people, creatures and gods of extinct races live in the ley lines, choosing never to return to visible existence. My Persian lover was swimming beneath me at the moment of my entry into the other world. I had not seen him before, but I was instantly projected into his arms. Extinct Persian men are a species of hairy males who are ten feet tall and have holes in the middle of their foreheads and earlobes through which cosmic energy flows. They are capable of lifting women into the air into any position imaginable, and every year their penises grow one inch and become more enduring. Air sex, like the mating of birds, is an addictive art form. With my Persian lover I could rise into the air like a helium balloon and trust the sky beneath me, the empty spaces in mind and body, the dreamless nights. I was initiated into the world of life after death, and I never returned to my house by the sea.

My followers of course spread the good news. I had ascended.

Secret Puissance

after Frank O'Hara

The professor kept smoothing his hair back from his forehead and talking about my lousy snow poems

when I picked up Frank O'Hara's book with a nude man on its cover. It was true that I rarely listened to a word the professor said. "Secret puissance," I read, translating it into pretty Jane's secret pussies and feeling in my crotch the tiny pressure of rain. I looked up nervously, wondering if the professor knew

that in Jane's secret pussies gorgeous blossoms, tigers, tongues and streams were yawning and stretching out their exciting flesh, and suddenly it was summer

by the sea. Did the professor feel the heat of the sand in his bathing trunks? No. Did he know he could perform miracles here? No, he was as perceptive as a rock. Exactly how do you fuck a rock, Frank O'Hara? I've loved so many rocks, and I'd really like to know

the veined man swinging from the vines while parakeets scream, the professor as an unmarried man in love with pretty Jane's secret pussies that call out to him: drop in sometimes. We're tired of being single. I looked back from afar

as the professor carefully slid his wire rimmed glasses back up his nose and adjusted his position over pretty Jane. She was crying plaintively and waking up at noon in a sunlit hotel room, still dreaming of her sophronitis rosea orchids

last seen in the hot-tranced instances of wetness, the delirious forest of my regard.

The Death of the Orgasm

Because it slept in your skin for years
because everything vanishes beneath its fingers
because yellow light is bleeding from its heart
because you and I are whispering and touching its soft skin
because it can hear the hollow clip of your footsteps in my empty
    streets
because we're falling behind it, becoming smaller, fainter, calling
    each other's names
because it is always looking for something else.

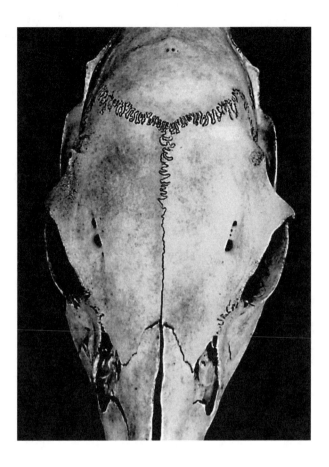

Orgasma skolta, the final orgasm; *skolta* derives from *skoltere*, L. to scald, scold, school of death; *skolitiri*, dirge dances; also *skolitro*, percussive musical instrument.

No one ever admits it, especially not you, whom *orgasma skolta* adores: how sometimes when you close your eyes, you can feel it like cold breath on your skin, like ghost fingers on your hair, your lips, the lobes of your ears, the nape of your neck —until it reaches the place behind the body where absence begins, holding you down like a spell, a drug, a longing for the one you can never have, should never love, your one aphrodisiac, though you always insisted there is no such thing.

Where Memory Ends

We've begun our disappearing act. It's our last scene. Nothing can be done about it. Gradually we become invisible to one another, then to the world. Just the other night a neighbor knocked on the door and said if I had even half a heart, I would give money to the March of Dimes. I thought of admitting I didn't have half a heart. After all these years I didn't even have a voice. Not that I haven't spoken. Only a short time ago, I screamed. At the top of my lungs. But to no avail. My voice, having lost its effectiveness, simply gave up. I've heard the voice is always the first thing to go among blond, blue-eyed WASPy woman who know that silence is golden. The mouth feels rather silly, opening and closing without forming words. Then the nose checks out, having no reason to smell what can never be tasted. The fingers become numb, no longer feeling the world at their tips. But the eyes and ears linger long afterwards, nostalgic, seeing and hearing what used to be. Gradually they see only dreams. Fantasies. Having lost touch with the world as it stands. Having reached the point in time where the orgasm ends.

Glossary of Selected Terms

abstraction: an orgasm seen from afar. A bird's eye view of an orgasm.

adagio: that moment after orgasms when everything is forgiven.

ant: an orgasm that bites, leaving tiny teeth marks in the skin.

bud: a folded orgasm.

caesuras: orgasms that wait in the background. Breathless orgasms.

collegno: an orgasm additive, commonly used to solidify orgasms.

deja vu: an orgasm that unexpectedly comes back to life. This can happen at any time or place.

ebb: an earthly orgasm, as opposed to flow, a divine orgasm.

embouchure: an incantation used to inspire or ward off orgasms. Oddly, the words are the same in both cases.

etc.: where certain, usually female, orgasms draw the line.

fantasy: an anthology of orgasms.

flesh: the landscape of orgasms.

gazette: one who can peer through the eyes of an orgasm.

guilt: the afterbirth of a Puritan orgasm.

halo: the orgasm of an angel.

Heloise, Anton: (1937-) an authority on the language of orgasms. His book, *Orgasms at First Sight*, can be found at a bookstore near you.

ins and outs: a psychological disorder marked by the propensity to describe one's orgasms at length.

Jacinth: the essence of orgasms. A perfume.

klister: the abyss separating man and his orgasm.

leitmotif: the process of having the same orgasm over and over again.

litotes: the language of discrete orgasms. Also, an orgasm with a broken wing.

lobscouse: the man who has lost everything, his house, his soul, his orgasms.

mirror: the orgasm of the unknown.

Nectaris: the study of the aesthetics of orgasms.

orgasm: the guest who comes too seldom. Also, a revelation.

phoenix: a seemingly extinct form of orgasm, formerly enjoyed by hyper-virile males.

poem: an orgasm that burns the lips. Also, slang for the female erogenous zone.

pro-: a prefix denoting the pre-orgasmic state of being, the time when one is conspiring secretly.

quell: the ability to quiet one's orgasms. This is especially important if one is to travel to those countries where the people have ceased to believe in orgasms. In such places, if people suspect you are having an orgasm, they will arrive in droves to study you as one might study a relic or an endangered species.

quintillate: what a body does when experiencing orgasm mania.

rallentando: the rule, no orgasms before noon, sometimes posted at sea-side resorts.

risk: a trial one must pass in order to attain the orgasm of the spheres.

shadow: an orgasm that fails to arrive. A sleeping orgasm.

Shradah: a slow dance, a sort of funeral rite for orgasms performed in solemn silence.

shrink: an orgasm who suffers from very bad archetypes.

solitude: the nostalgia for orgasms.

Tallgrab: an outdated device used by Catholics to inhibit orgasms in Victorian England. Protestants and Jews were known to shun the use of Tallgrabs.

tears: a human liquid, often caused by a river of orgasms or a lack thereof.

unlaid: true suffering.

ursine: a back-to-nature form of orgasm that will leave a new wound on your flesh every time. Beware of it, especially while taking solitary walks in the woods.

vent: the places in the body through which pleasure escapes.

waves: dreaming orgasms.

whirlabout: the title of the common theological debate about whether or not it is ethical to think of one person while giving an orgasm to another.

Xavier: an orgasm who wishes to be a saint.

xylic: a lady-killer; one who can hear the ticking of female orgasms.

Yima: a legendary poet who died at the age of 27 from orgasm overdose and grief. His odes to orgasms are still sung in Madrid.

zither: the study of the ethics of orgasms. Also, an orgasm that jiggles.

Zollner: a mythic and stellar orgasm, the first orgasm, the Adam, the prima orgasmia materia, the orgasm that contains all orgasms.

Zomba: the ultimate judge of orgasms. The only one who can answer the question, who has the most fun in the state of orgasm?